THE OFFICIAL QUEENS PARK RANGERS ANNUAL 2018

THIS BOOK BELONGS TO...

Name: Age:

Favourite Player:

MY 2017/18 PREDICTIONS...	ACTUAL...
QPR's Final Position:	
QPR's Top Scorer:	
Sky Bet Championship League Champions:	
Sky Bet Championship Top Scorer:	
Emirates Cup Winners:	
Carabao Cup Winners:	
Teams to be relegated: 18th	
19th	
20th	

A Grange Publication

Written by Francis Atkinson and Ian Taylor
Designed by The 16K Design Works

© 2017. Published by Grange Communications Ltd., Edinburgh, under licence from Queens Park Rangers. Printed in the EU.

Every effort has been made to ensure the accuracy of information within this publication but the publishers cannot be held responsible for any errors or omissions. Views expressed are those of the author and do not necessarily represent those of the publishers or the football club. All rights reserved.

Photographs © Rex Features   ISBN: 978-1-911287-78-0

CONTENTS

6	KITS THROUGH THE AGES
8	2016/17 PLAYER OF THE YEAR AWARDS
12	WHERE'S THE GAFFER?
14	100 YEARS AT LOFTUS ROAD QUIZ
16	FANZONE
19	SPOT THE BALL
20	SIX OF THE BEST
26	#QPR1718 KITS REVEALED
30	WORDSEARCH: QPR MANAGERS
31	SPOT THE DIFFERENCE
32	MANAGER PROFILE
36	#RSINPORTUGAL
38	PRE-SEASON
42	YOU ARE THE REF
44	JUST FOR STAN
47	WORDSEARCH: THE NO. 10 SHIRT
50	FIVE TALKING POINTS...
54	NEW BOYS...
60	QUIZ ANSWERS
62	FIXTURES 2017/18

KITS THROUG

AS MUCH AS ANYTHING ELSE, A FOOTBALL CLUB'S KIT AND COLOURS DEFINE THE CLUB IDENTITY; OFTEN IT IS THE REASON MANY OF US ARE ATTRACTED TO A TEAM IN THE FIRST PLACE!

Fans are very passionate about the kit - home and away strips are subject to much scrutiny from die-hard supporters. Kit launch is as an eagerly-anticipated event each pre-season as young and old get in line to be the first to sport the shirt of their heroes.

We have put together two posters this year as part of our **100 years at Loftus Road** celebrations which are here for your perusal. We hope you like them.

Special thanks to John Devlin, the architect of these pieces.

QPR Kits... 100 Years at Loftus Road

BOTH AVAILABLE AS POSTERS FROM THE QPR SUPERSTORE AND ONLINE.

THE AGES!

QPR Kits through the Ages

WHAT'S YOUR FAVOURITE?

BOTH AVAILABLE AS POSTERS FROM THE QPR SUPERSTORE AND ONLINE.

2016/17 PLAYER OF THE YEAR AWARDS

ALEX SMITHIES' IMPRESSIVE 2016/17 SEASON IN GOAL FOR QPR WAS REWARDED WITH THREE GONGS IN THE CLUB'S END OF SEASON AWARDS.

The R's number one was named Supporters' Player of the Year, Ray Jones Players' Player of the Year and Junior Hoops' Player of the Year.

Smithies was in inspired form over the course of the season, forging an ever-growing reputation for saving penalty kicks.

The keeper expressed his delight at scooping the awards treble, commenting: "It's nice to get some sort of recognition for the work you've been doing all season, so I'm really delighted to win all three awards.

"It always means a lot when your teammates vote for you and the fans have been fantastic with me since I arrived here, so the two awards they've voted for are special too.

"I've enjoyed the support I've received from everyone for my performances this season."

Elsewhere, Ryan Manning capped a fine breakthrough season by winning the Daphne Biggs Supporters' Young Player of the Year award.

Manning, who made his debut against Wolverhampton Wanderers on New Year's Eve, went on to make 18 appearances in the Sky Bet Championship, scoring one goal.

The 2016/17 Kiyan Prince Goal of the Season award went to Yeni N'Gbakoto for his stunning

free-kick against Birmingham City on February 18th.

Entering the fray as an 85th minute substitute with Rangers 3-1 up, N'Gbakoto set the seal on a stunning away win for the R's with a brilliant 30-yard free-kick at St. Andrews, as Ian Holloway's side ran out 4-1 winners.

Finally, A Kick Up The R's fanzine editor Dave Thomas was named Supporter of the Year. Thomas, a lifelong Rangers fan, celebrated his award in the 30th year of the popular fanzine, which continues to go from strength-to-strength, season on season.

Congratulations to all our winners.

GOAL OF THE 2016/17 SEASON

YENI NGBAKOTO V BIRMINGHAM CITY
18TH FEBRUARY 2017

WHERE'S THE GAFFER?

CAN YOU SPOT QPR MANAGER IAN HOLLOWAY IN AMONGST THE QPR FAITHFUL?

Answers on page 60

100 YEARS AT LOF

1. QPR played host to the Arsenal in the FA Cup in January 1921 in front of a Loftus Road crowd of 20,000. What was the score?
A) 1-0   B) 0-1   C) 2-0   D) 1-2

2. In that same match the boys from West London played in which shirt?
A) Blue and white hoops
B) All white shirt
C) Green and white hoops
D) Dark blue and light blue halves

3. In 1930, a Third Division South meeting with Swindon Town ended in a high scoring 11 goal thriller, what was the final score?
A) 8-3   B) 9-2   C) 7-4   D) 6-5

4. In 1948, in front of a bumper Loftus Road crowd of 27,500, QPR sealed their first-ever Championship and Football League promotion from the old Third Division South. Who were our opponents in the 0-0 draw?
A) Newport County
B) Swansea Town
C) Bournemouth
D) Brentford

5. QPR recorded their highest win at Loftus Road in December 1960 in front of a meagre 4,805 attendance, but how many QPR goals were the crowd treated to?
A) 8   B) 9   C) 10   D) 11

6. Loftus Road, August 10th 1968, Football League First Division. Who scored the R's first ever goal in the top-flight versus Leicester City in a 1-1 draw?
A) Mike Keen
B) Tony Hazell
C) Frank Sibley
D) Les Allen

7. In 1972 QPR played Nottingham Forest in W12 and the 3-0 home win was also notable for a special debut; whose was it?
A) Martyn Busby
B) Gerry Francis
C) Stan Bowles
D) Don Givens

8. Top-of-the-table Leeds United visited Loftus Road in the penultimate game of the 1973-74 season. The Champions won 1-0 in front of a record QPR home gate; what was the attendance?
A) 33,353   B) 34,353   C) 35,353   D) 36,353

9. QPR thrashed eventual champions Derby County at Loftus Road 4-1 during the 1974-75 season but something unusual happened before kick off - what was it?
A) Derby were late turning up
B) Derby manager Brian Clough was sent off before the match had started
C) A streaker ran onto the pitch
D) Derby had to wear the QPR away kit

10. A memorable 1975-76 season kicked off with a 2-0 home win over the almighty Liverpool on August 16th. Who got the first QPR goal which went on to win goal of the season?
A) Mick Leach
B) Gerry Francis
C) Stan Bowles
D) Dave Thomas

11. In that same glorious season QPR signed off at home with another 2-0 win against which famous opposition?
A) Chelsea
B) Arsenal
C) Leeds United
D) Manchester United

12. Stan Bowles had a remarkable European adventure in the 1976-77 season. What happened at Loftus Road and again in the away tie?
A) Stan was sent off in both legs
B) He scored an own goal in both games
C) He scored two hat tricks
D) He was carried off injured in both games

13. Stan again! The QPR legend scored his 11th goal in Europe during the 1976-77 campaign, setting a new British record for goals scored in Europe in one season. Who were the opponents in the home tie where Bowles set this record?
A) SK Brann
B) FC Cologne
C) Slovan Bratislava
D) AEK Athens

14. A sad ending to the 1978-79 season at Loftus Road as QPR were relegated to the second tier of English football despite winning 5-1 against Coventry City, but who brightened Rangers' spirits with a debut hat trick that day?
A) Mickey Walsh
B) Glenn Roeder
C) Paul Goddard
D) Clive Allen

TUS ROAD QUIZ

15 QPR v Luton Town, Football League Division Two, Loftus Road, 1st September 1981. This fixture was notable for what?
A) QPR kicked off with 12 players
B) Luton had to wear a QPR away kit
C) Terry Venables first match in charge of QPR
D) First ever match on an artificial surface in the football league

16 In 1984 the Loftus Road faithful were treated to arguably one of the West London clubs finest and most memorable comebacks. Was it?
A) 4-4 draw v Luton Town FC
B) 5-5 draw v Newcastle United
C) 6-6 draw v Watford FC
D) 7-7 draw v Charlton Athletic

17 Victories against Chelsea are always sweet but there is a stunning 6-0 victory on record. Which year was the Loftus Road thrashing dealt out?
A) 1984 B) 1985 C) 1986 D) 1987

18 In that same match a QPR player notched a superb hat trick. Was it…?
A) Wayne Fereday
B) John Byrne
C) Michael Robinson
D) Gary Bannister

19 Everyone remembers Trevor Sinclair's spectacular 'Goal of the Season' overhead-kick against Barnsley FC at home in the 1997 FA Cup tie, but what was the final score?
A) 1-0 B) 2-1 C) 3-1 D) 3-2

20 A 6-0 rout of Crystal Palace saved QPR from relegation to the Second Division on 9th May 1999. Who got a magnificent hat-trick that day?
A) Steve Slade
B) Kevin Gallen
C) Paul Murray
D) Chris Kiwomya

21 Most people will tell you that they have not heard noise like it inside Loftus Road. It was when Paul Furlong scored to put QPR 1-0 up on the night, 2-1 up on aggregate versus Oldham Athletic in the Second Division play-off semi-final second leg. What time did the goal go in?
A) 78th minute
B) 82nd minute
C) 86th minute
D) 90th minute

22 QPR had a superb 2010-11 season, finishing as Champions, but the unbeaten start to that historic campaign ended in December 2010 at the hands of which club?
A) Watford
B) Cardiff City
C) Leeds United
D) Leicester City

23 Another thrilling comeback in March 2012 which sparked the Premier League survival bid. From 2-0 down, the R's came back to win 3-2 with three late, late goals. In what order were they scored?
A) Derry, Cissé, Mackie
B) Cissé, Mackie, Derry
C) Mackie, Derry, Cissé
D) Cissé, Derry, Mackie

24 On their return to the Premier League in the 2011-12 season, a hostile atmosphere inside Loftus Road helped the hoops to a 1-0 win over arch rivals Chelsea. Who scored the winning goal?
A) Adel Taarabt
B) Akos Buzsaky
C) Tommy Smith
D) Heidar Helguson

25 Another joyous night in W12, this time in the play-off semi-final second leg against Wigan Athletic in the 2013-14 season. Which player won the penalty late, which Charlie Austin then converted to level the tie?
A) Bobby Zamora
B) Ravel Morrison
C) Joey Barton
D) Junior Hoilett

26 On QPR's return to the top flight for the 2014-15 season, who were the opponents for the opening home match, which the Hoops lost by a narrow 1-0?
A) Swansea City
B) Hull City
C) Sunderland AFC
D) Aston Villa

27 Which 'Hero in Hoops' notched a hat-trick in a 3-2 win at Loftus Road in December 2014 versus West Bromwich Albion?
A) Leroy Fer
B) Niko Kranjcar
C) Charlie Austin
D) Matt Phillips

Answers on page 60

15

QUEENS PARK RANGERS
FAMILY FANZONE

Visit the Family FanZone before QPR home matches at PlayFootball Shepherd's Bush!

The FanZone is open from 12pm to 2.30pm before Saturday home matches at Loftus Road that kick-off at 3pm. It will feature a range of fun activities throughout the season, including a speed cage, quick feet activity and face painting.

There will even be at least one first team player in attendance to sign autographs and pose for photos before most matches.

The Family FanZone is **FREE** and is open to all, even if you are not going to the match.

Come and join us this season!

HOLIDAY SOCCER SCHOOLS

During school holidays QPR in the Community Trust deliver their popular Holiday Soccer Schools at numerous venues across West London. Holiday Soccer Schools provide a safe and professional environment for children aged 5-14 to learn new and develop existing skills. Sessions are inclusive to all and allow children of all abilities to enjoy playing football regardless of their previous experience and make lots of new friends along the way!

WEEKLY SOCCER SCHOOLS

Weekly Soccer Schools take place throughout the school term during evenings and weekends. Our highly experienced coaches deliver fun and engaging sessions to players of all abilities aged 5-11. Each session is delivered with an emphasis on fun and engagement, with the technical aspects being developed during small-sided games with age appropriate questions, demonstrations and challenges.

ADVANCED SOCCER SCHOOLS

Designed for boys and girls aged 7-14 years old, the Advanced Soccer Schools are designed to offer higher ability players the opportunity to receive quality coaching in a professional environment, surrounded by players of a similar ability in order to aid in their development. The Advanced Soccer School programme also acts as a pathway into the QPR Academy Development Centre, with multiple players progressing into these sessions & beyond over the past 2 seasons.

MINI SUPERSTARS

Mini SuperstaRs is a fun introduction to football for 3-4 year olds, an ideal choice for parents who want to give their children a healthy and active start in life.

Developed in partnership with Early Years professionals and teachers, and ran by our specialist coaches, ensuring that all participants develop interpersonal skills and more as well as having fun with a football.

All of our football courses runs within the clubs Player Progression Pathway, put in place to support the identification, development and progression of players with the potential and aspiration to play for QPR Academy and Development Centres.

WWW.QPRSOCCERSCHOOLS.CO.UK

SPOT THE BALL!

THIS SEASON'S OPENER AGAINST READING RESULTED IN AN IMPRESSIVE 2 - 0 WIN FOR THE HOOPS OF W12.
Can you spot the ball in the below image from the opening day victory? What about in the bottom image from our trip to Norwich City's Carrow Road?

Answers on page 60

SIX OF THE BEST

ALEX SMITHIES

Having come through the academy of the club he grew up supporting, Smithies made his first team debut on December 5th 2007 for Huddersfield. He came on as a 76th minute substitute for the red-carded Matt Glennon during Town's 4-1 defeat by Southend United at Roots Hall.

His first full start came in the 4-0 defeat at Leeds United on 8th December, after Glennon lost an appeal against his dismissal and Town were refused permission to loan an emergency goalkeeper on the grounds that Smithies was registered as a professional.

Smithies became the first choice keeper for the remainder of the 2008/09 season and, after the arrival of manager Lee Clark, made the number one jersey his own.

Throughout the 2009/10 season, Smithies was the only player to play in each and every League and Cup game for Huddersfield. He made 48 starts, 17 of which resulted in a clean sheet for the Terriers. His contribution in helping Huddersfield to a final position inside the League One playoffs was reflected by him winning the club's Young Player of the Year Trophy.

In conceding just 56 goals in such a competitive campaign, he won both praise and admiration from many quarter, earning the Football League's 'Young Player of the Month' award in February 2010 along the way.

After playing over 250 games for the Terriers, Smithies signed for Queens Park Rangers in August 2015. The 27 year old has gone on to make over 60 appearances for the Hoops and is seen as one of the club's best signings over the last few years.

In the 2016/17 season, Smithies was in outstanding form throughout the whole campaign and became somewhat of a penalty kick specialist – saving three, including two against Fulham. He was deservedly voted as Player of the Season and was also nominated for two categories at the London Football Awards.

SIX OF THE BEST

RYAN MANNING

QPR beat off a host of teams to bring exciting prospect Ryan Manning to the club in January 2015. The Irish Under-21 international made 18 starts for the Under-21s during the 2015/16 season, finding the back of the net twice in the process.

In December 2016, Manning was given his debut away at Wolves and the midfielder performed admirably as the R's picked up their first win in six matches.

The Galway-born playmaker has since gone on to establish himself in the first team and the technically gifted left-footer signed a new long term contract in January 2017, just a few days after scoring his first goal for the club against Fulham in a 1-1 draw.

Manning is usually a central midfielder but showed his versatility towards the end of the 2016/17 season playing at left-midfield and, on occasions, left-back.

SIX OF THE BEST

GRANT HALL

Grant Hall arrived at Loftus Road from Tottenham Hotspur, but it was with his hometown team Brighton & Hove Albion that he made his professional debut. Born in Brighton, Hall joined the Seagulls as a scholar in October 2009.

He made his debut - and only appearance - for Brighton against Southampton in January 2012, before joining Spurs later that summer.

He captained the Lilywhites' Under-21 team in the latter stages of the 2012/13 campaign, and wore the armband in the Barclays Under-21 Premier League play-off final at Old Trafford. He made 19 appearances in that competition during the campaign.

He previously impressed during a loan spell at League One Swindon Town in 2013/14, making 34 appearances for the Robins, including 27 starts.

Hall joined the R's on the eve of the 2015/16 season and went on to have a stellar campaign, featuring 42 times and winning the club's Supporters' Player of the Year award.

He played 36 games during 2016/17, fluctuating between a holding midfielder and central defender.

SIX OF THE BEST

PAWEŁ WSZOŁEK

Born in Tczew, Northern Poland, Wszolek came through the ranks at Polonia Warsaw in the top tier of Polish football. His impressive performances on the wing did not go unnoticed by bigger clubs in European football. After reportedly turning down a move to Hannover 96 in the Bundesliga, Wszołek left Polonia Warsaw after 52 appearances and nine goals, joining Sampdoria in July 2013.

In his first season with the club, Wszołek notched up 19 Serie A appearances and netted in their 5-2 defeat to Napoli.

In 2015, Wszołek was loaned to fellow Serie A side Hellas Verona, where he made 29 appearances and was seen as one of the brighter sparks in a disappointing season, which saw the club relegated from Serie A.

The skilful winger, who can play on the left or right, made his international debut for Poland in a friendly against South Africa in October 2012. He won his second cap against England in a 1-1 draw, which was famously played 24 hours after the fixture was scheduled due to bad weather.

Wszolek joined QPR on loan on deadline day in the summer of 2016 and was one of the standout players during the 2016/17 campaign – constantly getting the better of his full back down the right hand side.

Much to everyone's delight, Wszołek decided to extend his stay in W12 and is now tied down to a long-term contract.

SIX OF THE BEST

MASSIMO LUONGO

Midfield playmaker **Massimo Luongo** has benefitted from playing regular first team football ever since a move from Tottenham Hotspur to Swindon Town at the end of the 2012/13 season. Australian Luongo first moved to England in 2011 to join Spurs, after playing youth football for APIA Leichhardt Tigers FC in his homeland.

Loan spells with Ipswich Town and Swindon (twice) followed, before Luongo transferred to the County Ground on a permanent basis at the start of September 2013.

He won many admirers during 85 league appearances for the Robins, for whom he scored 13 goals.

Luongo enjoyed a fine season in 2014/15, contributing six goals and eight assists as Town reached the League One Play-Off Final, only to succumb to defeat against Preston North End at Wembley. He was also voted into the PFA League One team of the year by his peers.

On the international stage, Luongo already has over 20 senior caps for his native Australia. He was part of their squad for the 2014 World Cup in Brazil and was recently named player of the tournament at the 2015 Asian Cup.

Luongo scored the winning goal against South Korea in the final as the Socceroos claimed a 2-1 victory to lift the trophy. His outstanding displays for his country led to him being nominated for the prestigious Ballon d'Or.

The Australian international penned a three year contract at Loftus Road in 2015 and featured 33 times for the R's in the 2015/16 season. He was arguably the R's most consistent outfield performer during the 2016/17 season – becoming a crowd favourite with the Loftus Road faithful often heard chanting … "He's magic you know, Massimo Luongo."

SIX OF THE BEST

LUKE FREEMAN

idfielder Luke Freeman spent his youth career with Charlton Athletic and Gillingham, where - at the age of 15 - he became the youngest-ever player to feature in the FA Cup.

In 2008, he made the move to Premier League side Arsenal. During his early days with the Gunners, Freeman gained Football League experience with Yeovil Town and Stevenage.

He would later sign for Stevenage, leaving the Emirates without making a First Team appearance. His impressive displays for Boro earned him a move to Ashton Gate - the home of Bristol City.

In his first season, with Freeman highly-influential, City did the double by winning League One and the Football League Trophy. He was credited with over 20 assists and was named in the 2014/15 PFA Team of the Season.

A regular for the Robins, the 24 year old left Ashton Gate for Loftus Road having made 121 appearances in all competitions, scoring 10 goals.

The central midfielder, who can also operate on the left, has been very impressive since joining QPR in January 2017, chipping in with two goals during the remainder of the campaign.

#QPR1718

QPR'S NEW-LOOK ERREÀ KITS FOR THE 2017/18 SEASON WERE UNVEILED IN LATE JUNE.

Following close consultation with Technical Partner Erreà, the kits provide a perfect mix of tradition and elegance, with clean cut lines, attention to detail and a modern style being the hallmark features.

The designs merge the history and tradition of the club with the most sophisticated style innovation and research, while also taking into account the tastes and opinions of fans.

In keeping with tradition, the home, away and third kits will feature the classic broad horizontal hoops, in blue and white, red and navy, and black and green respectively.

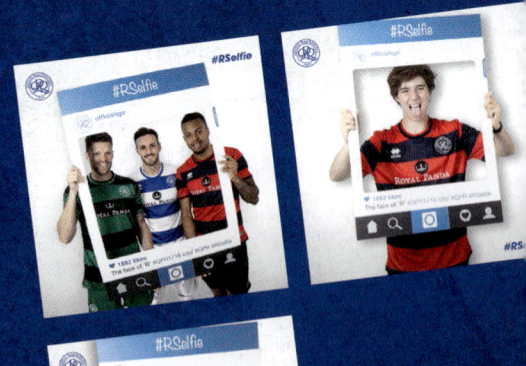

ITS REVEALED

HOME KIT

The three shirts, in highly breathable stretch fabric, have a round neck and semi-close fit. The shorts are in plain colours, while the hoops continue on the socks.

The red and navy kit provides an alternative to the Dennis the Menace design, while the green in the third kit offers a nod to the 100th anniversary of our time at Loftus Road, when the R's wore green and white.

AWAY KIT

QPR legend Stan Bowles was the first recipient of the new home shirt, with his former R's teammate Don Shanks and club ambassador Andy Sinton visiting him in Manchester to present him with the jersey.

Sinton told www.qpr.co.uk: "The kits look fantastic, and I am sure the fans will be delighted to see the hoops featuring across all three designs.

THIRD KIT

"It was a real honour and privilege to present Stan with the very first home shirt of the new campaign.

"He is widely regarded as the greatest player to ever pull on the blue and white hoops, so it is really fitting that he was given the first one."

QPR MANAGERS

CAN YOU FIND OUR FORMER R'S MANAGERS HIDDEN BELOW IN THE GRID? WORDS CAN GO HORIZONTALLY, VERTICALLY AND DIAGONALLY IN ALL EIGHT DIRECTIONS.

DICANIO
DOCHERTY
HOLLOWAY
HOWE
JAGO

MAGILTON
MANGNALL
MULLERY
REDKNAPP
SEXTON

SIBLEY
SMITH
STOCK
VENABLES
WARNOCK

Answers on page 60

SPOT THE DIFFERENCE

THERE ARE 10 DIFFERENCES IN THESE TWO PHOTOS. THE FIRST HAS BEEN CIRCLED, BUT CAN YOU SPOT THE REST?

Answers on page 60

IAN HOLLOWAY IN PROFILE

IAN HOLLOWAY IS BACK IN THE QPR HOT-SEAT, RETURNING TO THE CLUB HE SERVED AT BOTH AS A PLAYER AND A MANAGER WITH GREAT DISTINCTION.

Born on March 12th 1963 in Kingswood, Bristol, Holloway enjoyed a fine playing career spanning 19 years.

'Ollie', as he's better known, began his career at local side Bristol Rovers, coming through the youth ranks and making over 100 league appearances.

An industrious midfielder, Holloway moved to Wimbledon in 1985, but made just 19 league starts before moving on to Brentford.

His spell with the Bees was short-lived however, and after a loan spell at Torquay, he was soon on the move back to Bristol Rovers, making over 200 appearances between 1987 and 1991.

Loftus Road was his next port of call in 1991 – as the love affair with QPR began.

In five years in W12, he made 170 appearances, scoring five goals between 1991 and 1996.

He was also part of the Hoops team that famously won 4-1 at Manchester United on New Year's Day, 1992.

Renowned for his workman-like, gritty performances, Holloway was also a good distributor of the ball from the middle of the park. He played an important, disciplined role in the free-flowing Rangers team of the early-to mid-nineties..

He left QPR in the summer of 1996 and returned to, yes, you guessed it, Bristol Rovers for one final stint, which also kick-started his career in management.

Holloway would oversee 247 games in charge of the Gas, a spell which included an appearance in the Division Two play-offs.

QPR came calling in 2001, with Holloway taking over from Gerry Francis, who moved upstairs to become director of football at Loftus Road.

Rangers – already firmly up against it to survive when Holloway took charge – finished that season by being relegated to the third tier of English football. The club was plunged into financial administration and Holloway had to rebuild by recruiting a mixture of free transfers, trialists and non-league players.

The R's achieved an eighth-place finish in Division Two in 2001/02, followed by a fourth-place finish the following campaign, culminating in a 1-0 defeat against Cardiff City in the play-off final at the Millennium Stadium.

Undeterred, Rangers gained promotion as runners-up to Plymouth Argyle in 2003/04, and subsequently finished 11th in our first campaign back in the Championship.

Holloway parted company with QPR in February 2006, having firmly established the R's in the second tier – mostly on a shoe-string budget – and united the club in a way few managers have the ability and character to do.

After being linked with a number of jobs, Holloway re-emerged in June 2006 as boss of Plymouth Argyle, where he quickly established a rapport with players and supporters. After his first away win – a 3-2 victory at Sunderland – he memorably offered to buy a drink for all the 700 Argyle fans who made the 800-mile round-trip.

The Pilgrims finished 11th in the second tier in his first full season in charge.

With Plymouth in seventh place in the Championship in November 2007, Holloway resigned to join Leicester City, becoming their fifth manager in a turbulent season.

Having inherited a team threatened with relegation, he left the Walkers Stadium after narrowly failing to keep the club in the Championship.

Blackpool was his next port of call a year on and in his first full season with the Seasiders, Holloway remarkably guided the club to the Premier League with a 3-2 play-off final victory over Cardiff City. The success saw the Seasiders return to the top-flight of English football after a 39-year absence and Holloway became only the second Blackpool manager to win promotion in his first full season.

Blackpool provided fantastic entertainment in the Premier League during the 2010/11 campaign and recorded notable results, which included a league double over Liverpool. Yet despite Holloway's heroics, on the smallest budget in the division by a considerable margin, the club were relegated on the final day – even though they amassed a notable 39 points.

Undeterred, the following season saw Holloway guide the club to the Championship play-off final, where Blackpool narrowly missed out on an instant return to the Premier League after a 2-1 defeat to West Ham at Wembley.

A move to Crystal Palace followed in November 2012 and, once again, Holloway was back at Wembley at the end of the season, where his entertaining Eagles side were victorious after defeating Watford 1-0.

Holloway's spell at Selhurst Park ended in October 2013, however, after a difficult start on their return to the Premier League.

Following his appointment at Millwall in January 2014, Holloway went on to secure their Championship status for the 2014/15 season, guiding them from 21st to 19th. The Lions avoided the drop by four points.

He left Millwall the following season and has since enjoyed a productive career as a TV pundit for Sky Sports.

But now he's back where he belongs at Loftus Road – and has unfinished business to attend to.

33

JOEL LYNCH

#RSINPORTUGAL

The QPR first team squad enjoyed a productive seven day training camp in Portugal during pre-season, staying at the impressive Cascade Wellness and Lifestyle Resort in Lagos.

Under the watchful eye of gaffer Ian Holloway, the R's squad were put through their paces during the week-long camp, set in a unique cliff-top location overlooking the Atlantic Ocean.

The players completed three sessions a day for the majority of the tour, with a morning jog or swim getting the action underway.

After breakfast, a two hour mid-morning session in the beautiful Algarve sunshine would follow, before a final football session of the day at around 4.30pm.

With gym sessions and hill runs also thrown into the mix, it's fair to say the R's squad were pushed to their maximum during the opening week of pre-season.

PRE-SEASON:
R'S BEAT POSH IN PRE-SEASON

QPR STEPPED UP THEIR PRE-SEASON PREPARATIONS WITH AN ENTERTAINING WIN OVER PETERBOROUGH UNITED.

Jamie Mackie's 22nd minute opener gave Rangers the lead at the **ABAX Stadium,** on an afternoon where Ian Holloway was able to give no fewer than 23 players an outing.

Despite being pegged back by a Junior Morias double after the hour mark, QPR's youthful 'second half' XI responded well and ensured they were victorious thanks to goals from Jack Robinson, Ebere Eze and Charlie Owens.

The 120-minute match – split into four 30-minute periods – saw both sides field two entirely different XIs for each hour.

PRE-SEASON:
FC UNION BERLIN 2 - 1 QPR

RANGERS' PRE-SEASON WEEKEND IN GERMANY ENDED IN A NARROW DEFEAT, AS UNION BERLIN RAN OUT 2-1 WINNERS AT STADION AN DER ALTEN FÖRSTEREI.

Goals by Damir Kreilach (19th minute) and substitute Philipp Hosiner (penalty, 75) settled this friendly in the German capital, which was a rearranged affair due to the postponement following a waterlogged pitch 48 hours earlier.

But the R's far from disgraced themselves – and boss Ian Holloway, who saw Matt Smith draw his side level in the 48th minute, will no doubt be boosted by what was an improved display.

QPR's James Perch was forced into a goal-line clearance in only the second minute, but the match was a relatively even affair throughout.

Conor Washington saw his seventh minute blast beaten away by the home goalkeeper, before Union replied when Marcel Hartel's cushioned volley crept just over eight minutes later.

At the other end, Smith headed a hanging Perch cross wide in the 17th minute.

The hosts then edged in front. Kreilach's initial header was parried by Alex Smithies, before the same man hammered in the rebound.

Thereafter, chances continued to flow and, in the 32nd minute, Smith again went close with a header. Union's Felix Kroos then saw his free-kick deflect only inches over, before Ariel Borysiuk – who impressed for the R's – had his thunderbolt beaten away.

Rangers started the second half strongly and, after Jamie Mackie's blast was repelled by keeper Jakob Busk in the 46th minute, Smith eventually got his name on the scoresheet. He headed home Yeni N'Gbakoto's expert cross.

A deserved leveller but Union so nearly regained their lead 11 minutes later – Kreilach seeing his effort strike the post before trickling wide.

Smith's prodded attempt in the 70th minute was held well by Busk, before the home side settled the tie with a penalty, 15 minutes from time.

Perch was penalised for a high foot in the box, paving the way for Hosiner to decide matters from 12 yards.

Ultimately, a defeat for the Hoops – but reasons to be positive.

PRE-SEASON:
LOKOMOTIVE LEIPZIG 3 - 2 QPR

QPR SUFFERED A 3-2 DEFEAT AGAINST LOKOMOTIVE LEIPZIG IN PRE-SEASON FRIENDLY ACTION.

Ian Holloway's side found themselves 3-0 down after 51 minutes before goals from Ryan Manning and Paweł Wszołek helped them back into the match.

It was the hosts that took the lead after 11 minutes when Ryan Malone was on hand to finish inside the QPR penalty. A free-kick from the right hand side wasn't cleared and Malone shrugged off his marker to finish from close range.

Eight minutes later and Leipzig had doubled their advantage when Paul Maurer curled past Matt Ingram from just outside the QPR penalty area to make it 2-0.

Rangers responded and Reece Grego-Cox fired an agonising shot over the QPR bar following a good pull back from Paweł Wszołek.

QPR then went closer still when Luke Freeman's initial corner after 34 minutes hit the crossbar, before Grego-Cox headed Sean Goss's cross over on the follow-up as the first half ended 2-0 to Lokomotive Leipzig.

Following the break Holloway made the first of his changes, as Massimo Luongo replaced Sean Goss in the centre of midfield.

However, Leipzig extended their lead further in the 51st minute when Maik Salewski headed home after our hosts' initial effort struck the foot of Ingram's post.

Ryan Manning then reduced the deficit three minutes later with a well-executed volley from the edge of the Leipzig box. The Irishman created space 22-yards from goal with a nice swivel before half volleying past keeper Benjamin Kirsten to make it 3-1.

Moments after coming on, R's substitute Eberechi Eze almost made an instant impact for his side as he smashed Freeman's cross into the side netting from six-yards, before a series of Ingram saves at the other end kept the Leipzig attack at bay.

Then, ten minutes from time, QPR did manage to get the ball in the net again as Eze played in Grego-Cox but the R's youngster was flagged offside before Wszołek pulled back another goal for Rangers in the 83rd minute.

The Polish wideman cut in from the right before finishing well into the top corner with his left foot just inside the 18-yard box as QPR made it 3-2, but the R's were unable to grab a third as they suffered defeat in the Bruno-Plache-Stadion.

PRE-SEASON:
BOURNEMOUTH

RANGERS SIGNED OFF FOR PRE-SEASON WITH A 1-0 LOSS AGAINST PREMIER LEAGUE BOURNEMOUTH IN W12, ON A DAY WHEN THE CLUB PAID TRIBUTE TO ARGUABLY OUR GREATEST-EVER PLAYER.

A total of 9,386 fans witnessed this Stan Bowles Benefit Match at Loftus Road on Saturday 29th July, held in order to raise vital funds for QPR's iconic former number 10 in his fight against Alzheimer's disease.

The match doubled up as a pre-season friendly before the start of the new Sky Bet Championship campaign the following Saturday.

Ian Holloway's men were undone by a Jordon Ibe strike just prior to the interval, ahead of Reading's visit to the capital in a week's time.

Stan Bowles – flanked by former teammates Gerry Francis and Don Shanks – was given quite a reception as he led the two teams out before kick-off.

Visitors Bournemouth went close with less than a minute played.

The ball was eventually worked to goal-getter Josh King on 16 yards, but he blazed well over.

It was a lively start and Rangers were presented with a good chance of their own in only the fourth minute.

Matt Smith shot just wide from 12 yards, after the ball pinballed around the Bournemouth box.

The R's more than held their own against top-flight opposition early on, and spurned another notable opportunity on 11 minutes.

This time, Paweł Wszołek teed up Conor Washington on ten yards with a pinpoint right-flank cross, before the latter dragged his shot wide.

Chances continued to flow for Rangers thereafter.

Two minutes later, Smith also headed over from Luke Freeman's teasing delivery while, in the 24th minute, Mass Luongo slid in Washington to arrow a low 18-yard effort past the foot of the left-hand post.

Opportunities became less frequent as half-time approached – but the opening goal did arrive four minutes before the break.

Ibe cut in from the right before crashing a left-footed shot past Alex Smithies from ten yards.

Harsh on Rangers, perhaps, but they trailed at the interval nevertheless.

In contrast to the first half, the start to the second was a little slow.

R's boss Holloway then made some five changes just short of the hour mark and, a minute later – in the 58th minute – Luongo's 20-yard blast fizzed only inches over the crossbar.

At the other end, meanwhile, visitors Bournemouth really should have extended their lead in the 65th minute.

Both Ibe and Lys Mousset broke free of the Rangers defence and, when the former fed the latter, he forced a fine reaction stop from Smithies.

But chances were virtually non-existent after that, with QPR ultimately unable to overturn the half-time deficit in a disjointed second period.

Substitute Yeni Ngbakoto did go close to levelling matters with a free-kick in the final minute – his effort striking the left-hand post before replacement Cherries goalkeeper Aaron Ramsdale eventually sprawled to claim the ball.

YOU ARE THE REF

1 It is the last minute of injury time at the end of a match, the ball is in the crowd and they refuse to hand it back for the throw in to the opposition. The taker grabs the spare ball from the ball boy, takes the throw in and, just as his team mate heads it in, the original ball is thrown back into the area. What do you do?

2 A goalkeeper seems to make a world class fingertip save and is congratulated by his defenders - he even pumps the air - but as the opposition try to take a quick corner you are convinced that the keeper never actually touched the ball, your linesman isn't sure so what do you decide?

3 A striker is through on goal in a one-on-one with the opposing goalkeeper. He is pulled down but as you blow your whistle and signal for a penalty, you see the ball roll on into the net. What actions do you now take?

4 During an ill-tempered match, two opponents are hurling abuse at each other on the edge of the penalty area. Suddenly you notice the defender (who is just outside the area) spits at the attacker who is just inside the box. What do you do now?

5 The score stands at 2-2 in the dying seconds of a match and, as a shot comes flying towards your face, well off-target of the goal, you instinctively put your hands up to shield yourself. You are then horrified as the ball flies into the net. What now?

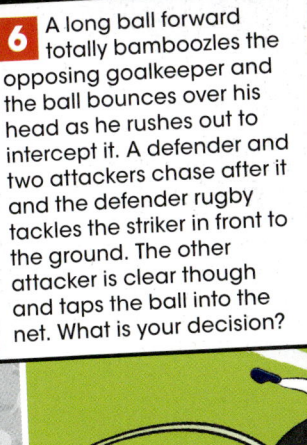

6 A long ball forward totally bamboozles the opposing goalkeeper and the ball bounces over his head as he rushes out to intercept it. A defender and two attackers chase after it and the defender rugby tackles the striker in front to the ground. The other attacker is clear though and taps the ball into the net. What is your decision?

7 It's a cup game and you are into extra time. The home team's star striker gets injured and can't continue. All the substitutes have been used so the home side has to play on with only ten men. They make it to the penalty shootout and the same star striker wants to take a penalty as he now says he is fit again as the injury has passed. Do you let him?

ANSWERS

1: If the original ball that is thrown back into the penalty box hasn't interfered with play in your opinion then you award the goal! If, however, the ball has interfered with play, you must disallow the goal. You need to be sure!

2: It is your decision, decide quickly and stick to it regardless of what the players and crowd think. If you think the goalkeeper didn't touch it then award the goal kick and not the corner.

3: Firstly, if you have blown the whistle and signalled a penalty then you must stand by that and not award the goal. Ideally, you should have delayed your decision when the incident happened and you could then have allowed the goal by playing the advantage. You should also send off the goalkeeper

4: Immediately send off the defender for disgusting behaviour and then award a penalty kick. Technically this is classed as a foul and as the contact (in this case the spit) made contact inside the area then it is a foul and, therefore, a penalty-kick. It is the same scenario as a sliding tackle where the slide starts outside the area, but the point of contact is inside the area.

5: You have scored the winner, as embarrassing as that may be. You need to calm everyone down and explain that the officials are part of the field of play as are the bar, goalposts and corner flags. The goal must stand!

6: Award the goal and then show a yellow card to the defender for unsporting behaviour. You cannot give him a red card as the other attacker obviously had a goal-scoring opportunity so, in effect, the defender didn't deny that goal-scoring opportunity. You correctly played the advantage and the goal was scored.

7: No, you do not. Only the players that finished the match may take penalties but what you do have to do is make the numbers even by instructing the other team to remove one of their penalty takers. If the player in question had come back onto the pitch before the final whistle at the end of extra time, he could have taken a penalty.

JUST FOR STAN

STAN BOWLES 10

The iconic number ten shirt been worn by some great names and true R's legends over the years - but nobody deserved that cherished shirt more than QPR maverick and fans' favourite Stanley Bowles.

Voted as QPR's greatest-ever player by the adoring Loftus Road faithful, Stan 'The Man' epitomised everything that the hooped number ten shirt stands for in W12 and stood out in the golden era of 70s flair players.

Not only was he a great team player, he was also gifted with incredible skill, vision and a left foot sweeter than Willy Wonka's Chocolate Factory!

Add to that the fact that he scored 97 goals in 317 appearances, as well as setting-up innumerable others, it is easy to see why Stan is held so dear in the hearts of the R's fans, his former team-mates and the footballing fraternity at large.

Also known for his gambling exploits and adventures with QPR team-mate Don (Mr Donald) Shanks, Stan was a friend amongst the supporters and people of a certain corner of west London, which hasn't been forgotten.

And so, when the pre-season benefit match was announced against Bournemouth to help Stan and the Bowles family in his fight against Alzheimer's, the cruel disease which has inflicted the R's legend, it came as no surprise that nearly 10,000 fans turned out in support with tens of thousands of pounds raised for his on-going care.

Stan gave so many of us endless, wonderful memories as a player and the benefit match was another wonderful day, the result of hard work and affection by so many.

Here is another little tribute, a selection of photos from the day and some old classics, to help remind us of the magic of Stanley Bowles ....

45

NEDUM ONUOHA

THE NO. 10 SHIRT

CAN YOU FIND THE QPR ICONIC NUMBER 10'S HIDDEN IN THE GRID? . WORDS CAN GO HORIZONTALLY, VERTICALLY AND DIAGONALLY IN ALL EIGHT DIRECTIONS.

BEDFORD
BOWLES
BUZSAKY
BYRNE

CURRIE
GALLEN
GODDARD

MARSH
STAINROD
WEGERLE

```
M W K Y K R M L G J F K
R W E W K V X C N T X D
L Q B G R A U R X J P R
W N O D E R S D F M L O
T E W Y R R O Z M M E F
K L L I M R L V U N P D
H L E H N W Y E R B R E
F A S I P X N Y C M T B
N G A C T L B X B D F Y
G T Q T G O D D A R D Q
S G X K Z L Z T H N M B
Z H S R A M R F D N K T
```

Answers on page 60

PERSONALISED QPR GIFTS

FROM £6.99

qprpersonalisedgifts.co.uk

MATT SMITH

49

FIVE TALKING POINTS...

WE LOOK AT THE FIVE MAJOR TALKING POINTS AHEAD OF THE R'S 2017/18 CAMPAIGN.

1 ON PAPER

On paper, at least, QPR have been handed a challenging opening schedule to the new campaign, facing three of last season's top eight (Reading, Sheffield Wednesday and Norwich) in our first five league games. The Hoops also host Hull City – who were relegated from the Premier League – early on.

2 THE 100TH ANNIVERSARY

In the year that QPR celebrate 100 years of playing at Loftus Road, our home clash against Ipswich Town on September 9th falls one day after the significant milestone of the R's first-ever match at our famous home. This should be a special occasion and certainly not one of the 23 home league games you'd want to miss!

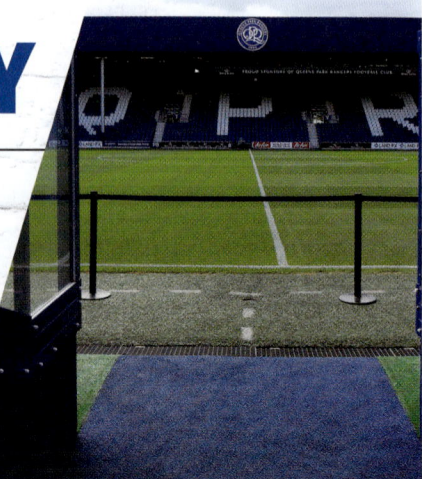

3 FIRST DERBY

Just a few days after the anniversary, we face our first London derby of the season against Millwall at Loftus Road. Let's not forget that Millwall were the last team that Ian Holloway managed. Later in September, we play Fulham at Loftus Road, but have to wait until the middle of November before facing our other west London rivals, Brentford.

4 CHRISTMAS IS KIND

The festive Christmas period has been relatively kind to Rangers supporters in terms of clocking up miles. Just before the festivities begin, we'll face Bristol City at home and then on Boxing Day travel to Suffolk to take on Mick McCarthy's Ipswich Town side – a round trip of just under 200 miles. A short journey to Millwall follows on December 30th, with Cardiff City at home being the first fixture of 2018.

5 SEASON FINALE!

Having been undefeated against Leeds United last season with one win and a draw, QPR will end the domestic league season in West Yorkshire on May 6th. The penultimate match of the season sees Ian Holloway's side host Harry Redknapp's Birmingham City at Loftus Road.

PAWEŁ WSZOŁEK

YENI NGBAKOTO

NEW BOYS

COMING DOWN FROM THE PREMIER LEAGUE

SUNDERLAND

MANAGER: SIMON GRAYSON
NICKNAME: BLACK CATS
STADIUM: STADIUM OF LIGHT
CAPACITY: 49,000
MILES FROM LOFTUS ROAD (ROUNDTRIP): 554
POSITION: 20TH

2016/17

The Black Cats had been flirting with relegation for a few years and came up short this term under David Moyes, finishing bottom of the table. They had previously performed great escapes to keep them in the division but will now have to rebuild as they look to make a quick return to England's most prestigious league.

ONE TO WATCH

Duncan Watmore – The forward sat out much of this campaign after he ruptured his cruciate ligaments and will be eagerly anticipating getting back on the pitch. Watmore has shown himself to be a fast and tricky forward who will no doubt trouble many defences in this division once he returns to full fitness.

MIDDLESBROUGH

MANAGER: GARRY MONK
NICKNAME: THE BORO
STADIUM: RIVERSIDE
CAPACITY: 33,746
MILES FROM LOFTUS ROAD (ROUNDTRIP): 504
POSITION: 19TH (PREMIER LEAGUE)

2016/17

Boro were reasonably strong defensively but scored the least amount of goals in the division and that proved their downfall as they were relegated with manager Aitor Karanka leaving the club in March, and interim Steve Agnew failing to turn their fortune around. Ex-Leeds United gaffer Garry Monk was appointed their new manager in the summer and will hope to guide them back to the Premier League at the first time of asking.

ONE TO WATCH

Rudy Gestede – The target man may have struggled to adapt to the Premier League but at this level remains one of the most difficult opponents in the division due to his power and aerial ability. If Middlesbrough can provide him with the right kind of service, then you can expect him to be a hit for Monk's side.

HULL CITY

MANAGER: LEONID SLUTSKY
NICKNAME: THE TIGERS
STADIUM: KCOM STADIUM
CAPACITY: 35,450
MILES FROM LOFTUS ROAD (ROUNDTRIP): 428
POSITION: 18TH (PREMIER LEAGUE)

2016/17

Hull left it a little too late in their quest to stay in the Premier League and were ultimately relegated on the penultimate weekend of the season. The Tigers began the campaign with a win over Leicester City but began to fade badly under Mike Phelan. Marco Silva took over and oversaw a really impressive second half of the year where they were particularly strong at home, but in the end it was not quite enough to get the job done. Leonid Slutsky has since taken over, with the Russian undertaking his first job in English football.

ONE TO WATCH

Sam Clucas – The 26 year old was arguably Hull's most impressive midfielder last season and seemed to be the player that made everything tick. The Tigers will be hoping they can keep their midfielder who has proved to be so vital for their team in recent months.

NEW BOYS

COMING UP FROM LEAGUE ONE

SHEFFIELD UNITED

MANAGER: CHRIS WILDER
NICKNAME: THE BLADES
STADIUM: BRAMALL LANE
CAPACITY: 32,702
MILES FROM LOFTUS ROAD (ROUNDTRIP): 320
POSITION: 1ST (LEAGUE ONE)

2016/17

After enduring a slow start to their League One campaign things began to pick up for Chris Wilder's side around October and from that moment on there was no stopping the Blades. United were simply too powerful for the rest of the teams in the division and their attacking style of football saw them finish well deserved champions, clocking up 100 points.

ONE TO WATCH

Billy Sharp – The forward once again showed his goal scoring prowess in League One this season topping the scoring charts with 30 strikes. The Yorkshireman is undoubtedly Wilder's talisman up top and will likely be heir main goal scoring threat in the upcoming campaign.

BOLTON WANDERERS

MANAGER: PHIL PARKINSON
NICKNAME: THE TROTTERS
STADIUM: THE MACRON STADIUM
CAPACITY: 28,723
MILES FROM LOFTUS ROAD (ROUNDTRIP): 436
POSITION: 2ND (LEAGUE ONE)

2016/17

Phil Parkinson's side were pretty consistent throughout most of this season and ended the campaign deserved runners up despite Fleetwood pushing them all the way. Known more for their defensive qualities – Bolton conceded fewer goals than any other team during League One this season - they had, in David Wheater and Mark Beevers, a very solid central defensive partnership.

ONE TO WATCH

Josh Vela – The 23 year old can operate in a number of positions and is perhaps Bolton's most eye-pleasing player, but he also chipped in with ten goals this season and Parkinson will be hoping he can make the step up to the next level.

MILLWALL

MANAGER: NEIL HARRIS
NICKNAME: THE LIONS
STADIUM: THE DEN
CAPACITY: 20,146
MILES FROM LOFTUS ROAD (ROUNDTRIP): 22
POSITION: 6TH (LEAGUE ONE)

2016/17

Millwall began this season very slowly by their own high standards and at the turn of the year it looked highly unlikely that they would reach the play-offs. But an excellent run of form in 2017, which included nine clean sheets and a positive run in the FA Cup, saw the Lions sneak into sixth place. They defeated Scunthorpe in the Play-Off semi-finals and were then the surprise winners against Bradford in the final.

ONE TO WATCH

Lee Gregory – After regularly finding the net in the last two seasons in League One, Gregory will want to prove that he can do it at a higher level. A scorer of all types of goals, his partnership with Steve Morison was vital for the Lions in securing promotion.

2017/18 QPR KIT
AVAILABLE NOW

AVAILABLE FROM THE QPR SUPERSTORE OR AT WWW.SHOP.QPR.CO.UK

LUKE FREEMAN

QUIZ ANSWERS

100 YEARS AT LOFTHUS ROAD QUIZ (P14-15)

1. (C)
2. (C)
3. (A)
4. (B)
5. (B)
6. (D)
7. (C)
8. (C)
9. (D)
10. (B)
11. (C)
12. (C)
13. (A)
14. (D)
15. (D)
16. (B)
17. (C)
18. (D)
19. (D)
20. (D)
21. (B)
22. (A)
23. (A)
24. (D)
25. (D)
26. (B)
27. (C)

WHERE'S THE MANAGER? (P12)

SPOT THE BALL! (P19)

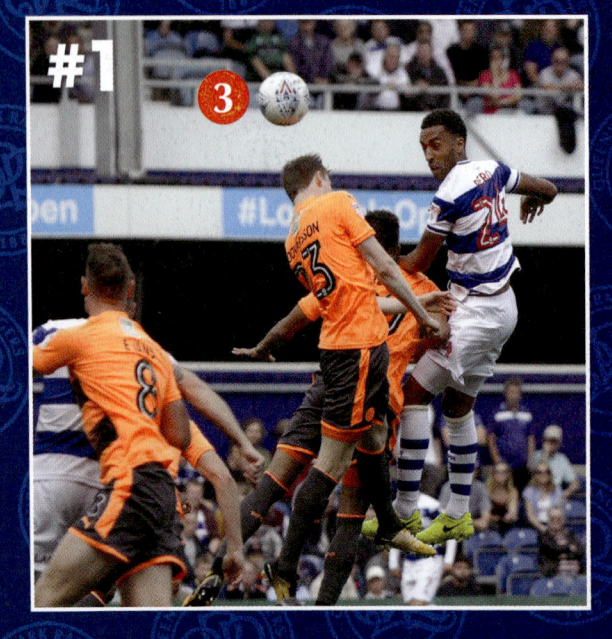

#1 — 3

#2 — 5

QUIZ ANSWERS

SPOT THE DIFFERENCE (P31)

QPR MANAGERS (P30)

THE NO. 10 SHIRT (P47)

FIXTURES 2017/18

2017

AUGUST

8th August 7:45 PM
Northampton Town (H)
Carabao Cup

12th August 3:00 PM
Sheffield Wednesday (A)
Championship

16th August 7:45 PM
Norwich City (A)
Championship

19th August 3:00 PM
Hull City (H)
Championship

22nd August 2:45PM
Brentford (H)
Carabao Cup

26th August 3:00 PM
Cardiff City (A)
Championship

SEPTEMBER

9th September 3:00 PM
Ipswich Town (H)
Championship

12th September 7:45 PM
Millwall (H)
Championship

16th September 3:00 PM
Middlesbrough (A)
Championship

23rd September 3:00 PM
Burton Albion (H)
Championship

26th September 7:45 PM
Barnsley (A)
Championship

29th September 7:45 PM
Fulham (H)
Championship

OCTOBER

14th October 3:00 PM
Sunderland (A)
Championship

21st October 3:00 PM
Bolton Wanderers (A)
Championship

28th October 3:00 PM
Wolverhampton Wanderers (H)
Championship

31st October 7:45 PM
Sheffield United (H)
Championship

NOVEMBER

4th November 3:00 PM
Nottingham Forest (A)
Championship

18th November 3:00 PM
Aston Villa (H)
Championship

21st November 7:45 PM
Derby County (A)
Championship

25th November 3:00 PM
Brentford (H)
Championship

DECEMBER

2nd December 3:00 PM
Preston North End (A)
Championship

9th December 3:00 PM
Leeds United (H)
Championship

16th December 3:00 PM
Birmingham City (A)
Championship

23rd December 3:00 PM
Bristol City (H)
Championship